Undiminished Returns is a deeply satisfying collection of poems— formally, psychologically, and spiritually. Charting the pilgrim path with candour and with a cadence and rhythm which capture the spirit as well as the body of being a believer, Jeremy W. Johnston opens up the private world of deeply held faith in a way which is at once unaffectedly personal, and touchingly universal. There are echoes here of Herbert, Bunyan, and Hopkins, all flowing into an original voice whose range can convey to us the grandeur of God, the sorrow of sin, and the fearful beauty of salvation in Christ Jesus. These are poems to turn the heart heavenwards, pieces which both capture what is easily seen, and highlight what is easily missed in Christian spirituality. These poems are a joy to read, and will be returned to again and again for their lyricism, thoughtfulness, and God-glorifying focus.

ANDREW ROYCROFT, *poet, blogger at thinkingpastorally.com, and pastor of Millisle Baptist Church in Northern Ireland*

It is in the very nature of poetry that it offers undiminished returns. You can return to the same poem over and over and find that it is richer and has more to offer on each return, indeed one poem, in the midst of such returns, often generates another. So it is with this fine collection from Jeremy W. Johnston; he has returned us to the classic form of the sonnet and taken inspiration from the likes of George Herbert and Christina Rossetti, and in doing so he has crafted a collection of beautiful and thought-provoking new poetry. This return to formal verse is not a repetition but a renewal.

MALCOLM GUITE, *poet, musician, Chaplain at Girton College, Cambridge, and the author of numerous books of poetry and prose, including Sounding the Seasons, After Prayer, and Mariner: A Voyage with Samuel Taylor Coleridge*

What does it mean to believe and be haunted by doubt? Or to doubt yet be haunted by belief? Johnston's poems, evidence of a life steeped in words and the Word, give voice to a secular condition ill-at-ease with our freedom and autonomy from God. In an age of irony, Johnston's direct, sincere voice provides one healing word after another.

DOUG SIKKEMA, *a regular contributor to Comment magazine and assistant Professor of English and Core Humanities at Redeemer University*

It has been said that the strength of poetry lies in its ability to communicate beyond the strict transfer of information; to write or read a poem, then, is to trade in the language of the heart. In our own determinedly heartless age, it is no surprise to find that such modes of expression are increasingly neglected. So it is with much enthusiasm that I commend *Undiminished Returns* to the reader's careful thought and reflection. Johnston's sonnets are written from the treasury of his own experience—though those expecting either forays into spiritual triumphalism or morbid introspection will be pleasantly disappointed—and have been arranged to reflect the varied seasons of Christian pilgrimage. I encourage both believer and non-believer to pick up and read this deeply human and Christ-immersed volume.

BENJAMIN INGLIS, *pastor, writer, editor at benjamininglis.com, and director of Blind Bards Literary Society*

This book is all that a book should be, starting with its marvelous title. Johnston's poems are devotional poems of the highest order, meeting the essential criteria of fixing a reader's thoughts on the spiritual life and (as Milton put it) setting the affections in right tune. A particular strength of the collection as a whole is its arrangement of the Christian life according to a chronological principle, tracing life in Christ from its beginning to its consummation. The book offers additional riches as well. The personal reflections at the beginning and close of the book are engaging and instructive. The quotations from famous Christian writers that are scattered as epigraphs throughout the book are priceless. The book sparkles with a sense of authorial attentiveness to every detail.

LELAND RYKEN, *professor emeritus of English at Wheaton College, literary editor of the ESV Bible, and the author/editor of over fifty books, including The Liberated Imagination: Thinking Christianly about the Arts and The Soul in Paraphrase: A Treasury of Classic Devotional Poems*

I am often asked how to read poetry and what poetry to read. I will recommend *Undiminished Returns* to all who wish to expand or even just begin their understanding and appreciation of poetry. By including an educational introduction and selections from history's great poets, this collection of original poems—written in a variety of forms and about significant themes—is a veritable course in poetry. Even more, the verses within form a beautiful, poetic exploration of a soul in pilgrimage.

KAREN SWALLOW PRIOR, *author of On Reading Well: Finding the Good Life through Great Books and Fierce Convictions: The Extraordinary Life of Hannah More—Poet, Reformer, Abolitionist*

JEREMY W. JOHNSTON

UNDIMINISHED
RETURNS

Poems of a Christian Life

H&E
Publishing

Undiminished Returns: Poems of a Christian Life
Copyright © 2020 Jeremy W. Johnston

H&E Publishing, Peterborough, Ontario
www.hesedandemet.com

Cover Image: Expulsion from the Garden of Eden Painting by Thomas Cole, 1828
Cover design by Chance Faulkner
Interior font: Equity

Paperback ISBN: 978-1-989174-61-6
eBook ISBN: 978-1-989174-62-3

Dedication

To my sons and daughters,
Joseph, Nathanael, Katherine, & Abigail

"I do not cease to give thanks for you,
remembering you in my prayers,
that the God of our Lord Jesus Christ,
the Father of glory, may give you the Spirit of wisdom
and of revelation in the knowledge of him... "
Ephesians 1:16–17

"...It is not yet enough. So I must try,
In my poor turn, to help you see it too..."
    —*from* "And Is It Not Enough?" *by Malcolm Guite*

"Dear deep well of speech and silence
 of words
 and space between words
 [...]
 Teach us gladness
 Teach us lightness of heart
 Surprise us"
    —*from* "The space between words" *by John Terpstra*

"...it is when I turn to Christ, when I give up myself to His person-
ality, that I first begin to have a real personality of my own."
    —*from* Mere Christianity *by C.S. Lewis*

CONTENTS

Surprised by Poetry:
Confessions of a Reluctant Poet

"That soul that can reflect upon itself, consider itself, is more than so."
    —*from* "Meditation XVIII" *by John Donne*

"I envy no man's nightingale or spring,
    Who plainly say, *My God, My King.*"
    —*from* "Jordon (1)" *by George Herbert*

Surprised by poetry

Poetry has been a big part of my life.

My first poetic influence was my mother. Although English is not her native tongue, she regularly wrote English poems when I was a child, and many of those poems were printed in the Poet's Corner of our local newspaper. She taught me to delight in wordplay and capturing life with lyrical language. Growing up in a Christian home also filled my Sunday mornings with the beautiful poetry of hymns, choruses, Scripture, and even the occasional poet preacher.

In school, I studied poetry—like so many others—from kindergarten through to my university English degree. I memorized poetic verses to woo the woman who is now my wife, and as an educator, I have taught poetry for nearly twenty years to eager (and not so eager) students. I also regularly read poetry for pleasure, for comfort, and, yes!—for illumination.

Poetry has been a big part of my life.

What I never fully imagined was that I would write poems as well. Before this point in my life, the closest I ever came to writing poetry was when I was a kid: I "wrote" a poem for a last-minute Mother's Day card, which turned out to be mostly plagiarized from the Bard. Having forgotten to buy a card for my mom, I raided the bookshelf in my father's study for inspiration. With a few minor tweaks, I copied out a choice passage I found in Shakespeare's *King Lear*.[1] Not surprisingly, my ruse was easily uncovered. Since then, I have relied—less surreptitiously—on Hallmark cards as a proxy for endearing words of affection to my loved ones.

So what kept me from picking up the pen and crafting my own poetry? One reason was that the kinds of poetry I enjoy and teach are mainly poems by dead poets. Being "dead" is not a morbid prerequisite to appear on the course syllabi of the English courses I teach;

---

[1] I cannot remember the exact passage I "borrowed" from the Bard, but I suspect I copied out one of the speeches spoken by Lear's loquacious and fawning daughters, Gonerill or Regan (Act 1, scene 1). Ironically, their speeches, though meant as paternal flattery, were really insincere—as the rest of the tragedy clearly reveals. I am sure, however, that I *meant* every word to my mother, plagiarized though those words were!

I do read, value, and teach living poets too. It just happens that the kinds of poets I relish most are from bygone eras, poets like Shakespeare, Milton, Donne, Herbert, Bradstreet, Herrick, Blake, Coleridge, Rossetti, none of whom made it to the 20th century. Despite my penchant for old, dead poets, I believe that poetry, like all art forms, must be continually created and shared. My reluctance for writing poetry was not that the world didn't need new poets, but rather, does the world need the kind of poetry I would write? In many ways, we tend to write what we read, or, perhaps, what we want to read.

This leads me to the second obstacle making me a reluctant poet. I never thought that poetry was a medium best suited *for me* to engage audiences. As a teacher by trade, I am predisposed to saying something clearly to my students (or at least I try hard to do so). Poetry, on the other hand, is rarely clear—at least at first glance. Poems often require re-reading and careful reflection. Poetry, by nature, is often nuanced, sub-textual, and enigmatic. This is why, as a writer, I have opted for prose—essays, articles, columns, blogs. It never occurred to me to attempt (in a serious way) to write poetry to say the things I wanted to say. I confess that I resisted writing poems because I knew that I would be too precise, too obvious, too didactic. I felt my work would have the ring of an advertisement at best or propaganda at worst, only fit for inspirational wall plaques at the local Christian knick-knack shop. There is a place for this kind of writing, but it wasn't the kind of writing I wanted to do.

Why poetry, why now?

So why am I now writing poems to say the sort of things I want to say? The first reason is that poetry has been a significant influence on my spiritual growth and edification. In particular, the devotional poems of George Herbert, John Donne, and Christina Rossetti often have a "stark clarity" unseen in modern poetry, yet they are rich and rewarding. I have also been blessed by the vibrant poetic prayers and liturgical poems from church history, such as the Anglican *Book of Common Prayer*. There is value in verse that is both lucid and lyrical. In his poem, "Jordan (1)," Herbert defies his fellow poets' penchant for convoluted verse by arguing for clarity: "is all good structure a winding stair? [...] Must all be veil'd, while he that reads, divines, catching the sense at two removes?"[2] Reading poetry doesn't have to resemble ascending (or descending?) a staircase designed by M. C. Escher. Like Herbert, I believe there is room for good poetry that clearly speaks to the reader.

The Bible is also known for its perspicuity —that is, its accessibility and plainness. This is especially true of the Book of Psalms. Though easy to understand, the poetry of the psalms powerfully impacts readers. Rarely do psalms require extensive exegesis or elaborate commentaries to glean great insights about God and our relationship with him, as well as insights into our far-ranging emotional landscape. A single reading of a chapter can make our hearts sing, yet there remains a deepness in the Book of Psalms, which will require all eternity to plumb their depth fully. This is why we read psalms for worship, for funerals, for weddings, for comfort, for courage, for delight. Meaningful yet clear poetry matters to us in the ups and downs of life. Christ, in agony on the cross, quotes poetry from the Book of Psalms, which reveal how poetry can powerfully capture and convey our most unsettling and heartfelt pain. Beyond the Book of Psalms, there is rich poetry scattered throughout the Bible, such as beautiful prayers and songs, well-crafted aphorisms, and poetic prophecies. The Apostle Paul, who is known for his elongated prose, not only quotes frequently from the Psalms as well as from Gentile poets, but he also embeds his own poetry in a few of his letters.[3] We are told that "all Scripture is breathed out by God and profitable for teaching, for reproof, for correction, and for training in righteousness, that the man of God may be complete, equipped for every good work" (2 Timothy 3:16–17). The presence of so much poetry in the Bible underscores both the usefulness of poetry and the immense value of *clear* and *meaningful* poems in equipping the saints.

Beyond the Scriptures, we have a heritage of nearly two thousand years of rich Christian poetry. It seems that as long as saints have

---

[2] George Herbert, "Jordan (1)" in *The Temple* (UK: Penguin Classics, 2017), 76.
[3] See, for example, Colossians 1:15–20; Philippians 2:6–11; 1 Timothy 1:17, 3:16, 6:15–16; 2 Timothy 2:11–13.

breath in their lungs, words on their tongues, and ink in their wells, every generation and every place continue to produce new Christian poets, artists, and storytellers. New creators are always required to speak to and about each new generation.[4] This is because art powerfully shapes, as well as reflects, our world. Poems help us to make sense of our own time and place. Although truth doesn't change, times and situations change, as do metaphors and language; this is why there will always be a need for new creations of one kind or another to present old truths in new ways.

What strikes me the most, however, is that poetry impacts us in a way no other form of communication can. Scholar and professor Leland Ryken notes that "poetry is a way of thinking."[5] Poetry is a way of seeing the world and making sense of the world. The experiences that inhabit life seem chaotic and disjointed; poetry has a way of arranging the pieces and revealing the meaning of these seemingly random moments in life. This is why reading and writing poetry has been such a great help to me and so many others, especially as we reflect on God's surprising and mysterious workings in our Christian pilgrimages.

An encounter with living poets

Having experienced the spiritual and life benefits of *reading* poetry, it is no surprise that my clarity about *writing* poetry started to come into sharp focus when I had the opportunity to read Christian poetry by 21st-century poets. One such poet is John Terpstra, an award-winning Canadian poet and author. I met Terpstra when he served as the Writer-in-Residence at the school where I teach. The man, like his poetry, plays with words and ideas in a fresh and uncompromising way. His poems are born out of "every day" and "everywhere" life, yet uniquely capture "a day" and "a place" and "a life." When reading his poems, one cannot help but hear what

---

[4] See "Gifted for such a time as this" in Jeremy W. Johnston, *All Things New: Essays on Christianity, culture and the arts* (Kitchener: Joshua Press, 2018), 37–39.

[5] Leland Ryken, *A Complete Handbook of Literary Forms in the Bible* (Wheaton: Crossway, 2014), 153.

Terpstra has to say; he does *say* something to his readers. He achieves this without being preachy or prescriptive. His poems awaken me to my surroundings, my faith, and the rough and tumble realities of my soul. His poetry also rouses me to the power of subtlety and plainness as well as artfully arranged words and thoughts. His work has influenced the few poems in this volume where I play with free verse form (although in no way comparable!). Terpstra writes about the real world, here and now, and he writes honestly and openly about the reality and challenges of faith in our present context. His humble and authentic voice is immanent in the words printed on the page. At times it feels as though he is softly speaking his poems over my shoulder. Perhaps it helps that I know John because I can hear his voice and cadence in the ears of my mind. Such is the benefit of reading living poets!

Another living poet who enflamed my interest in writing poetry for "such a time as this" is Malcolm Guite, an Anglican priest, Cambridge chaplain, educator, poet, musician, and Hobbit-like sage. I have enjoyed his work on various social media platforms, and I recently read through his collection of sonnets called *Sounding the Seasons*, a poetic pilgrimage through the ecclesiastical calendar. This year, I also happily journeyed through his collection *After Prayer,* and as I write this, I am about to start his book *The Singing Bowl.* I first encountered Guite's poetry in 2017 during a visit to the beautiful city of Cambridge, England. Someone had placed a poem by Guite inside the *Church of St Edward King and Martyr.* At the foot of the historic pulpit of Hugh Latimer, an English Reformer, I read a small placard with a sonnet capturing the martyr's ministry as he preached here during a tragic and unsettled time in church history. In those words, I found a poet who not only spoke for our time but spanned time and place, mixing words with the wood and stone of history. Guite's masterful use of the sonnet—the form of poetry I cherish the most—has been a vital influence on my poetry. One day I hope to come close to emulating his style. I am inspired by Guite's contemporary adaptation of the sonnet form as well as his use of the kinds of religious and metaphysical poetry Donne and Herbert penned three centuries ago. Like Malcolm Guite, I also share a love for Donne and Herbert. Just as these saintly poets wrote for their

7

time, Guite writes for our time, and we continue to need new poets to write for all time. We see this not only in poetry, but in the wonderful offerings of modern hymns created by writers such as Keith and Kristyn Getty, Stuart Townend, and Matt Redman. Musician and songwriter Keith Green is another saint, though now in glory, who points me toward writing verses that present God and his gospel to our current world.

Indeed, writing songs and poetry about God is inexhaustible! As much as I love and cherish the old hymns by Watts, Wesley, and Crosby and the old poems by Herbert, Donne, and Rossetti, there is ample room for contemporary voices and contemporary words about the glory and wonder of the Lord Jesus Christ. So though I was a reluctant poet, I began to see there was not only room for new poems, but also a need for new poets.

Write the books you want to read
In this texting, tweeting, digitally distracted culture, I have found grounding and great refreshment in the incarnated letters and words of poems on the written page. Poetry often accompanies my daily morning meditations in prayer and the Word. I can testify to the tremendous value of reading the poetic and spiritual reflections of fellow sojourners. My quiet times with the Lord are enriched daily by these poems and prayers.

Likewise, many of the poems collected here in this book are written as devotional poetry. Some of my poems are prayers; some are reflections on a given theme or moment in time. All of the poems are written to do what the poetry of Terpstra and Guite—as well as many other poet-saints—have done for me: to bring pleasure, comfort, and illumination. C.S. Lewis once remarked that authors should write the books they want to read.[6] Indeed, this is why I set out to write this book of poems: it is the sort of book I enjoy reading and

---

[6] In a letter to his publisher, Lewis writes, "I wrote the books I should have liked to read if only I could have got them. That's always been my reason for writing. [...] No rot about 'self-expression'" quoted in Chad Walsh, *C.S. Lewis: Apostle to the Skeptics* (Eugene: Wipf & Stock Publishers, 2008), 2.

would like to keep reading. My prayer is that there are enough readers out there who feel the same way about my poems, and will benefit from them as much as I did in writing and reading them.

A call to write old truths in new ways

On his deathbed, George Herbert gave the manuscript of *The Temple* to a friend for publication. Herbert hoped that the poems "may turn to the advantage of any dejected poor soul."[7] He begins his collection of poems with a whimsical address to his reader:

> Hearken unto a Verser, who may chance
> Rhyme thee to good, and make a bait of pleasure:
>   A verse may find him who a sermon flies
>   And turn delight into a sacrifice.[8]

This country parson, preacher, and poet humbly suggests that verses from his book may, through the "bait of pleasure," reach hearts and minds where a sermon may not. The hope is not merely to delight the reader but to "rhyme thee to good." Many saints who have read Herbert's *The Temple* testify to the good that it has done them. C.S. Lewis read and re-read the poetry of George Herbert and counted *The Temple* among the top ten most influential books on his life.[9] Although I am far from being a master wordsmith like George Herbert, I hope that many will be blessed by reading this collection of poems about the Christian life. There are indeed many enriching poems, hymns, and songs already written; yet, I humbly add my lyrics to the

---

[7] John Piper, "He Saw God Through His Pen: George Herbert (1593–1633)," *Desiring God*, March 1, 2020, www.desiringgod.org.

[8] George Herbert, "The Church Porch," in *The Temple* (UK: Penguin Classics, 2017)

[9] When Lewis was asked "What books did most to shape your vocational attitude and your philosophy of life?" he listed *The Temple* as one of his top ten books (see, Colin Duriez, *The C.S. Lewis Chronicles*, New York: Blue Ridge, 2005). In a couple of personal letters, Lewis called Herbert's poetry the "sweetest of religious writing" (letter to Mrs. Arnold, 26 December 1951) and "extremely nutritious" (letter to Mrs. Margaret Gray, 9 May 1961).

"smörgåsbord" of offerings. Our infinite God is worthy of endless praise.[10] All the poetry in human history has yet to scratch the surface of who God is and what he has done for us. There is infinite space for more. I was encouraged in this endeavour by John Piper, who is also a poet as well as a preacher. He writes in his essay "God is not boring" that

> Imagination is like a muscle. It grows stronger when you flex it. Imagination is also contagious. So I suggest that you hang out with people (mainly dead poets) who are full of imagination. Then labour to say an old truth in awakening ways. God is worthy. "Oh sing to the Lord a new song" — or picture, or poem, or figure of speech.[11]

As a writer, I believe that I'm called to "labour to say an old truth in awakening ways." This is what I have attempted to do with this book. Through the verses, metaphors, and rhymes of this assortment of sonnets and poems, my hope is that the Lord would use my words to edify, exhort, encourage, uplift, and bless you, the reader.

---

[10] The Psalmist asks a rhetorical question: "Who can utter the mighty deeds of the Lord, or declare all his praise?" (Psalm 106:2). The answer: no one (other than God himself) can "declare *all* his praise." We will have all eternity to declare God's beauty, truth, and goodness, and to praise him for his wondrous deeds!

[11] John Piper, "God Is Not Boring," *Desiring God*, February 26, 2003, www.desiringgod.org.

How to Read this Book

Far be it from me to dictate how you should read this book. My only desire is that as you read it, you experience delight, encouragement, exhortation, and perhaps some measure of illumination. That said, I would like to reveal my poet's heart and my authorial intent as I wrote this collection of poems.

I'm drawn to stories about "the journey." One of my favourite novels is J.R.R. Tolkien's *The Lord of the Rings*, which is about an unlikely hero's epic journey from the comforts of home to the desolate and despairing domain of evil itself. I have enjoyed reading and teaching epics like *The Odyssey, Beowulf,* and *The Epic of Gilgamesh*— all tales involving quests of one kind or another. John Bunyan's epic allegory, *The Pilgrim's Progress*, the beloved story of a Christian's journey from the City of Destruction to the Celestial City, has perhaps meant the most to me in my Christian walk. So it is no surprise that I arranged this collection of poems to echo the pilgrimage of a Christian. To reflect this spiritual journey, I organized the poems in chronological order from unsaved to saved, capturing the various seasons of life and culminating in ageing and death. This is why I recommend that you begin at the beginning and experience the pilgrimage of faith mirrored by real life.

Although I have drawn from my own life experiences, I have not written these poems as a memoir or autobiography. I have attempted to convey feelings and thoughts anyone might have in a life of faith, what it's like when a Christian knows peace and joy and when he or

11

she struggles with sin and doubt. In all stages of the Christian life, I have contemporized the persona to reflect contemporary readers, who I hope will read—and benefit—from these poems. The most challenging aspect was capturing the voice of a soul dead to Christ. My aim was to avoid creating a "strawman" caricature of an unbeliever, but rather to convey genuine lostness. I hope I succeeded. My prayer is that these poems will encourage readers to *remember* who they once were and *know* who God is making them into (Ephesians 2:12-14; 1 Corinthians 6:11). Most importantly, I hope and pray that you will gain a richer and deeper knowledge of Christ himself.

Prologue
king of infinite space

"I could be bounded in a nutshell, and count myself a king of infinite space, were it not that I have bad dreams."
—from Hamlet (II.ii) *by William Shakespeare*

A king of infinite space

Tightly bound, sealed in a small nutshell:
Here, I am a king of infinite space.
There's no more. No light, no heaven, no hell.
I knew not, would not know, another place.
My world in a nutshell—still, he broke in,
broke me out—crushing pressure, a great crack,
scattered pieces, all is shattered, broken.
Then I saw that life's no longer pitch-black.
Shell-shards now rest upon a warm, soft palm.
My broken life is new life. There is more,
this is more. I've been longing for a psalm
to sing, a word to walk, all unlooked for,
yet here I am in a boundless dwelling.
He is the Infinite, he is the King.

Part 1:
Before Conversion
Winter sleep,
restless sleep

"Here we may reign supreme, and in my choice
To reign is worth ambition, though in hell.
Better to reign in hell than serve in Heav'n."
—the lost Archangel, *from* Paradise Lost, *by John Milton*

dead winter

Lostness. I thought they were lost.
Sightless. I knew there wasn't anything I wanted to see.

If ice could speak
       then what would it say.

If snow could walk
       then where would it go.

When I was dead
       what did I really know.

White Lie

So, it's the Winter of my contentment.
The bliss of my ignoring, neglecting
Neverminding. Asleep, softly snowing,
frost bit but I feel no bite. Resentment?
Yes, maybe, surely. I am indifferent.
White wind, whiteout, whitewash, white ice-piercing
contentment. Tomb cold. There's no begrudging—
I am certain that warmth is abhorrent.

Still, my marrow aches for comfort and heat.
I thirst for the thaw that cannot exist.
Feeding on ice yet groaning for a meal.
"All lies," I lie. "No water, bread, or meat!"
"Only blizzards, hail, and sleet," I insist.
My words, frozen breath: "only cold is real."

A winter feast

I gaze upon frozen grey earth and grey
sky. I can imagine holly, but never
have I seen it. Trampled tracks go astray,
away, nowhere. Leading me forever
yet never to hearth and home. Winter cold,
no bells heard. Cheer may come: this wispy dream
keeps me trudging. "Be merry," I've been told.
"Keep moving!" But with each step, my feet seem

to slip back, slip backward—I shout, "Forward!"
Stumbling feet, ice entombed, joyless marches.
What help is above? A circling buzzard
awaiting a cold dish. The bird watches,
waits, as I wane, to feast on my carcass.
It's always winter, but never Christmas.

I, Misanthrope

(It's been said)

I am created in his own image,
and I exist by his will. Formed, fashioned,
knit by divine, loving hands. He portioned
gifts to me, my heart, my mind, my courage

(I've been told)

He delights in me, such a privilege!
Child of God who's rescued and transitioned
from hopeless to hopeful, who's commissioned
to love, be loved—at least that is the "pledge"—

But I know.
            Humanity is over-
rated, over-populated—cancer.
The world's suffering is "humanity."
The planet's curse, polluter, destroyer,
Just a cosmic fluke, that's doomed to expire.
Good riddance, pestilence, good riddance me.

All I Know

All I know is that I don't want to know.
This is all there is. Nothing's going on.
I'll be forgotten, I'll forget when all's gone.
I've heard of God, but I don't care. Follow
me? I'd rather not. I'll go where I go.
I am free. Not your will, but mine be done.
I clock my miles on a wild treadmill run
Alive in the present is all I know.

So I refuse to bow to your tyranny.
I wisely cling to apathy, I want nothing more:
Love and lordship? That dish I won't try.
You can't feed the dead. You can't make me see.
I won't ask, not knock, not open the door.
I'm certain—I think—all truth is a lie.

Cosmic fraud

Is religion a hoax, a cosmic fraud,
for weak wills, simple minds, wishes unchecked?
Is god really real, are you really God?

It's said that you made the sky, stars, seas, sod—
made all things, all living things, all perfect.
Silly religious hoax, this cosmic fraud.

A book—riddled with errors, deeply flawed—
unquestioned "truth" from heaven sent direct.
Is god really real, are you really God?

Unbelievable belief, overawed
and easily duped, man's freedom is wrecked
by this religious hoax and cosmic fraud.

There's that far-fetched claim: on earth, he trod,
a resuscitated demigod! I don't expect
this god is really real, that you are God.

Some tale that's complex and completely odd,
a grandiose lie. But while I reject
this religious hoax, this cosmic fraud,
what if you're really real, *what if* you're really God?

Defy, Defile

I will make a covenant with my eyes
to gaze upon a virgin. There is no
god above, no god only Google—so
I consume digital skin, free from lies
of watching eyes. Now seeking new highs,
glazing, grazing each triple X video.
Lurking the browser set incognito—
Fake guilt branded "sin"... Yet something defies
my defiant stance. Who is really there?
Alone but not alone. Smart watch? Smart phone?
It knows my steps, my beating heart, where I
went, who I know... Yet someone, just and fair,
seems really there, counting each hair, each bone,
each breath. My heart knows, yet I still deny.

Her porn

(She is dreaming) In my dreams, I take or am taken.
A fantasy of words, an illusion
of love, a Harlequin tale mistaken
for real. I'm dazzled (or dazed?) by my confusion:
what do I want and what should I want.
I've seen images. I've been curious.
I'm intrigued/horrified by violent
crass sex. Simmering, dirty, furious.
I hate him/her yet desire him/her. Validate me,
but I don't need validation; desire
me, want me, seek me, but leave me be—
Fired by lusts of mind, burned by the fire.
I'm torn between what I'm supposed to be
and reality—Is this liberty?

Not really fair

My wish is that I would really belong—
to be at home here, to fit in somewhere.
I'll be whoever, I'll like whatever song,
I'll laugh right along, accept any dare.
A true friend, a real love, a kindred soul:
this is what my heart pines for, dreams about.
Alone in my loneliness, far from whole,
a shard of clay, a puzzle piece left out.
Is there no one like me, no one who likes
me? No not one. Not really. I'm alone.
Comfort sought in pints, warm lips, picking fights.
Dazed by TV, smokes, skin mags, joys on loan.
Why do I yearn for what's not really there?
Life—a so-called gift—is not really fair.

Symposium I:
Dear preacher

I feel that I'm generally a good
person. Better than most (in general).
I'm mostly kind to most people I should
or would be kind... Most people, but not all.
Some I ignore, some I dislike, some I—
I hate. Rightly so, as everyone says.
I'm a *very* good guy (at least I try).
I say and do what is right, so long as
I'm seen. If a man sins in a forest
and no one sees, it's not really a sin.
Why, then, do you tell me I must confess?
That God saves me from the trouble I'm in?
Dear preacher, I think you misunderstood:
I'm good enough, and I've done enough good.

Symposium II:
Dear soul

Dear soul, you say you believe there's a god
but not religion's god—shoved down your throat;
that every Christian you meet is a fraud
only wanting money to sustain the hoax—
preaching not practicing, wolves in disguise.
(You add) The church overflows with haters and crooks.
The Bible's just an old book filled with lies.
You won't be reeled in by bait and fishhooks.
So you say. But how do you know what's good, what's not?
You long to be loved and known, truly known.
You sense he's there, he speaks, yet you've not really sought
him. Burdened, lost, guilty, in pain, alone.

silence

Your heart knows it's true; let me call your bluff.
Dear soul, only Jesus is good enough.

Common Grace

Even at the close of day
the eye of heaven sees and helps us see,
flooding the world with warmth, light, and life.

An artisan, who delicately touches each sliver of grass,
each leaf, each stone, each granule of earth
Varnishing everything with light,
with gold and with beauty.

The green and red and purple are still green and red and purple
though endowed with a precious yellowy hue.
Even shadows become beautiful—
accenting, accentuating, amplifying.

All things are new
the ugly asphalt, street light pole, discarded soda can,
overhanging wires, cracked concrete, the wandering waste bin

gilded with gold
illuminated with love

This is an uncommon yet common grace
We all see and feel and know we need the sun.
That we would all see and feel and know our need for the Son.

Undone

Eyes slammed shut. There is no such thing as light.
Delusional, deceptive, half-formed hope.
A juvenile joke, fake news. I have sight
(though I refuse to see). I reach, I grope
I stumble, I step—I stay. Eyes held shut
by granite fists—fists ready to fight light
to bend the light, to tear the light, to gut
the luminescent lie. These eyes tied tight
by self-sewn thread. These eyes, my eyes will not
see. Not look.

      Yet my heart—it hopes there's light—

stupid, silly, foolish fable! I fought
hopeless hope. "No light!" I knew it was night.

But at night, a moon glows, something does shine.
Dawn may come. I may see.
                 Light may be mine.

Part 2:
No Mere Interlude

"And in the days of those kings the God of heaven will set up a kingdom that shall never be destroyed, nor shall the kingdom be left to another people. It shall break in pieces all these kingdoms and bring them to an end, and it shall stand forever"

—Daniel 2:44

No Mere Interlude

No mere interlude but the turning point.

So broken, so He broke in. Upset
    the disorder. Divine Descent: What child is this?

    Love Comes Down, Love Nailed Up, Love Laid Down
    Love Rises Up, Love is Lifted Up, Now Love Lifts Up.

    Morning has broken.

Part 3:
Christ Enters In
The Discontinuity

"Jesus said to him, 'I am the way, and the truth, and the life. No one comes to the Father except through me.'"

—John 14:6

Seeing the Unseen
After Colossians 1:15-20

Invisible God in visible flesh,
Eternal Eldest, High King, rightful heir.
Pre-womb, pre-tomb, maker of all things, fresh
from scratch—all galaxies, stars, atoms, and air,
nations, states, thrones, and all foundations laid.
Angels we have heard on high, he made too.
Nothing was not made by him who's unmade.
All things designed and built by him and through
him, for him. With nail-pierced hands, he still holds
the universe together—sustainer,
starter, death-killer: glory he enfolds
in sinew and blood. Although he's no sinner,
of such, his body is now made: redeemed
by his blood, at peace, and highly esteemed.

Wrath

God, a fuel-less fire yet consuming flame.
His Voice, a flashing light, a roaring sky,
trembling earth, rippling stone, wobbling mountain:
a word of judgment from the Lord Most High.
The universe is kindled, God's anger
will come, his Wrath will wage war with wayward
daughters, wicked sons. Foolhardy stranger,
hater of good, doer of wrong, downward
determined, deserving of death. Yet justice
is met—*but*—not by me. How can it be?
Love poured out, mercy given and restless
souls satisfied. Who bore the wrath for me?
The God-man, who came, not fire from above.
The God of Wrath is also God of Love.

Mary

Mary had a choice. "Be it done to me."
There's always a choice—deny, forget, run
away, stay, obey. Options are many,
even from the beginning—"Avoid one
tree, eat not its fruit. Choose any other,
delights of every kind." So she chose
to reach out, not look up, the *Mother
of All Living*; she chose thorns, not a rose.
But the *Favoured One*, she wondered with fear
while hiding so much in her heart. "Nothing
is impossible with God." Her call, clear,
Mary chose to receive what God would bring:
Seed to branch, crown to thorns, the bloom that dies...
Mary's fragrant rose would also arise.

A real baby

The baby Jesus could not speak a word—
he, who is the Word made flesh, blood, and bone.
A mere bleating lamb is the Good Shepherd.
The babe could not even walk on his own,
he, who walked on water and carried a cross.
Baby Jesus could not feed his stomach,
he, who is Bread, fed thousands without loss,
abounding fish and loaves from a child's snack.
The baby could not rule, though governments
sit on his shoulders. The child needs saving
from a jealous king... Saviour needs parents'
rescuing. This baby needs everything,
even though he made all things. How could he,
so willingly, set aside his glory?

THE CYCLE OF THE SHEPHERDS
I. The Shepherd

The unbending earth always feels comfortable
after an infinite day of walking and work.
Sheep and men shift and shuffle as we settle
in. Shadows and star-speckled blackness lurk
above, revealing nothing less than my empty
void. Disappointed in me —my parents
were, are. They hoped for so much more for me—
No one searched after my disappearance.
I am now a herder of sheep. And a thief.
Strange that the things I value least are the things stolen.
But nothing is ever free, except for grief,
and I'm rich in grief. Feet throbbing, legs swollen,
can't take another step—not even for double pay,
just endlessly waiting for another day.

THE CYCLE OF THE SHEPHERDS
II. The Angel

Such is God's way—the most important word
sent to men of least importance. So I came—
flash of light, glimpse of glory—to men and herd.
Terror tore at each one, along with shame.
"Don't be afraid," I said. "I bring good news."
Words like "great joy" and "all men" are foreign
to shepherds' ears who walk in scorn and abuse—
rough, wind-scorched men who know only sorrow and sin.
Now I see why he sent me here, to them.
Unto them, for them, as one of them: he came.
The Messiah is here in Bethlehem!
How he loves the poor, the sick, the lame!

They're the ones who know well what they really are

"Glory to the repairer of all that's broken;
Hear now! With this babe, your God has spoken!"

THE CYCLE OF THE SHEPHERDS
III. The Mother

So much mystery, yet so much misery:
Fear of shaming, divorce, death. A woman
with child, conceived of God? What blasphemy!
Thoughts of betrayal and tears of a good man.
Making matters worse, the census and journey,
the weight of God in my belly and on my heart.
Weary and wondering what the angel
meant for me, for us—what will be our part?
No room in the world where my baby could
be born—yet, shooting pain, the need to push—
with blood and water, my child has come to do good.
As I wrapped him, they came with an inrush
of pungent smells, wafts of outside, sweat, wool.
"Angels, we heard, peace, joy!" My heart is full.

THE CYCLE OF THE SHEPHERDS
IV. The Lamb

When we came, it was just as we've been told.
We heard the cry, coming from the stable,
not a bleating lamb but a baby to hold,
wrapped in a feed-trough used as a cradle.
His Father will be well-pleased: his child will
be the Shepherd—not because there's nothing
else he can do, but because there's nothing
else we can do—this child, bound, laying still.
An army of angels, white as stoked flames,
told us to come and see: no one believes us,
but I believe. I look up. I see the stars
no longer the void. Break of day means hope for us.
We praise God and tell all who will listen:
"This Lamb of God is our Shepherd of men!"

An even greater shift

Exiting Israelites plundering gold
from Egyptian masters—gentile gold made
into ark, altar, lampstand, table laid
with showbread, tent-tabernacle to hold
the symbols of God. With. Us. Now we're told
Orient Magi, star-gazers who payed
honour and praise, gave three gifts to the babe.
These gifts, no longer plundered, given gold
willingly in worship to the true God,
God with us, perfect tabernacle, tent
wrapped in flesh. King's gold crowns the star-led search.
Frankincense, a priestly gift. But most odd—
myrrh, embalming resin, with pungent scent.
He brings us in through the holy curtain rent.

The Word that Walked

He is more than an unmoved mover. He
is moved by compassion—by love—he wept!
Yes, wept real tears of brine: warm, wet, salty.
He walked, he healed, he laughed, he ate, he slept.
These aren't words in books, penned by an author...
What poet ever ate his own ideas?
What wordsmith writes with real light? Whoever
walked on soil he laid, soil he made? Jesus—
He entered in. Let that sink in. With us
He entered in. That One Word became words,
His Story became history. Jesus,
ink turned to blood, blood became wine, his hurts
no mere notion: rusty nails, rough-hewn wood
The Author's pain for our eternal good.

A Cruciform King

Crown Him King.
The King of kings,
The Lord of lords.
Crown Him with
a crown of wood,
whips, and thorns.
This is your King.
His Rule spreads far and wide—the Lord who Loves, the Lord of Love: this is Love.
As far as the east is from the west, from sea to sea, from nail to nail, His Love covers
cleanses, and clears, so we can come in, commune, be comforted, be rightly ruled! We are
spared by His not sparing. Yes, He spared no expense: costly gifts for newly made kings.
Clothed in regal,
wine red dripping
Royal Robes,
now White with
Righteousness.
His Ruling Rod
an unbroken reed.
Maker becomes
Meeter, God be-
comes Man, Regis
becomes rejected.
Alone yet elevated,
all can see. The Oak
adorned with blood
-sap, hung on cypress,
cedar, and pine tree.
A dais for The Death.
Power to live, power
to die, power to live
again. Cast away His
crown, so we cast our
crowns. Crown Him.

Wounds that heal

Dead as a Roman nail—water and blood
poured from the pierced side (made for our transgressions).
A corpse covered in gore: sweat, tears, blood, mud—
Dead body brought down (for our transgressions).
Body bathed in myrrh, incense, but not gold:
wrapped in a shroud and placed in a new tomb.
Stone was rolled, sealed and secure; guards were told
to watch a grave—so what did they see? Whom
will they blame? Angels and light, rolling rocks?
He left death behind, folded on a shelf.
The third day has come, so go tell that fox,
He ran the course, defeated death itself.
Holes in his hands, his side, his wounds revealed.
But now by his stripes we are surely healed!

THE RESURRECTION CYCLE
I. Eden Returning

It was the dawn of a new day, new week,
a brand new world, yet they came to the garden
to mourn their return to a graveyard Eden.
No angel barred their way, not this time: "Whom do you seek?" —
Wrapped in snow and piercing light, no sword drawn.
"He is not here, for he has risen! Come,
see the place where he lay," he welcomed them.
They looked: cloth, folded shroud—but body gone!
He's been taken! "But don't you remember?"
asked the angel. "Words spoken by the Living Word?"
Yet she wept. Death still stung. Hope still seemed interred.
But then they remembered, a glowing ember:
On the third day, our man, our God, Jesus—
he will rise and bring Eden back to us!

THE RESURRECTION CYCLE
II. I saw, I believed

Mary's report shattered our shattered hearts.
I thought there were no pieces left to break,
no room for more pain, no hardships left to take.
We—we must see, though hope is torn apart.
I got there first but I dare not enter in.
I expected rot and decay, a pale corpse
desecrated and humiliated within.
But I looked: folded linen, scent of myrrh...
Peter ran past, down into the black vault.
This prison has been abandoned, defied
not defiled; no defeat but a counterassault.
The binds of death have been neatly untied.
He's gone, he isn't here, we weren't deceived.
So I went in, I saw, and I believed!

THE RESURRECTION CYCLE
III. Soul Gardener

Sand scraped inside her throat from the weeping.
Her thoughts beat against her skull. Swollen eyes.
No relief. No joy. No hope left keeping.
A saviour had come: now salvation dies.

The garden, blooming with death, is well-tended.
A polished sepulchre, just an empty
Eden, a broken love, a paradise ended.
Then she saw a man, a gardener by a tree.

"Woman, why are you weeping? Why are you searching?"
She whispered, "Where is he?" Then he said: "Mary" —
He knew her, now she knew him — "Don't tarry,
go tell my brothers that I've seeded this sod
with eternal blossoms for our Father, our God"

Pilate reads the news

The seed of woman and a son of god?
Sounds sordid. Jupiter at it again.
This charlatan demigod is a cult-leader fraud!
Yet superstitious priests, so jealous and vain,
riling up the rabble against this fake
king, this vagrant babbler with a motley crew.
I'll release a rebel for mercy-sake,
mollify the mob shouting: "Kill this Jew!"

Now—hands are washed, crowds are gone, my job is done.
The man is dead, new week begun. What news?
The morning tabloid headline reads: "Dragon
Slayer Slain while Slaying Snake!" I peruse.
"Thieves rob cult leader's grave, the body snatched!"
Stolen corpse? Risen Lord? A hoax is hatched...

Elegy of the Resurrected

Walking the road to Emmaus, not the road
to victory, liberty, just dead-end
misery... No rescue, no overthrow,
no oppressors oppressed, no throne mended.

Though it's a bright morning, mourning eyes see only
a dim and fading day, an ashen road,
growing shade, feelings of fear and folly.
Drained hearts, empty hands yet a heavy load.

Regrets, wasted joy, misunderstandings.
Misguided certainty, unfounded faith.
Now the confused pilgrims talk of disbanding.
Christ wasn't Christ; hope is gone without a trace.

The two men walked, yet they stumbled with words.
Nothing makes sense. But then a man (neither knew)
came alongside them, asking, "What's on your mind?
What are you discussing? Why so downcast?"

The men with sallow cheeks, red eyes, rent hearts,
stood still, mouths agape: "Are you the only
one who's in the dark? Must be from foreign parts—
Jerusalem is awash in anguish

rife with grief... A prophet, powerful in word
and deed, was betrayed and crucified.
We longed for a redeemer, now hope's deferred;
his grave is robbed, body gone—pierced hands, side,

the man has died, yet there's women who claim
he lives and... and they *even* spoke to him—
to Jesus, alive! Is this truth or some con game?"
They glanced down with shame and unrelenting pain.

The man asked: "Have you neither seen nor heard
the things this man did, the truth this man said?
Listen to Moses and trust in God's Word,
The Christ must suffer, die, and rise from the dead!

"Remember the first gardener: with great
peace and promise he began his first day.
Delighting in God and his lovely helpmate,
living in bliss until he went astray...

"The wages of sin is shed blood and death.
Expelled from the Garden, man's exiled from love,
enslaved and lost, from birth to last breath.
All are desperate and cut off from God above.

"Sacrifice must be made to make right the wrongs,
to make unpure pure, unclean clean—for a time.
But all the seas brimming with blood
could not cover, cleanse, or cure men of their first crime.

"A new Adam is needed, a new way and new door —
A perfect man, a good man, a holy lamb.
The Tabernacle became the offering,
God with us became the One who died for you.

"He's a better Noah, washing judgement away,
He's Abraham's ram who took Isaac's place,
He's Joseph, whose brothers sought to betray,
sold for silver yet pays back love and grace.

"Remember David, the giant slayer
the man after the heart of God, poet,
warrior, musician, man of prayer,
favoured king—such high hopes yet he ruined it:

"Adulterer, murderer, passive father—
he could not reconcile love for his sons
and justice for wrongs. He did not bother
to punish or redeem—Tamar, Amnon,

"O, Absalom—though he loved his enemies
he could not save any, not even one.
But Christ is David's Lord, he's the remedy,
the everlasting king, the One who has won.

"He satisfied justice, he satisfied love
He enslaved the master, he freed the slaves
He went down, and now he's risen above,
High King of Heaven, Earth, and empty graves.

"He's the Passover Lamb, whose blood-stained posts
guarded against death and marked God's own sons.
'He was despised, and we esteemed him not,'
said Isaiah, 'the stone of stumbling, offending rock...'"

So this man explained the symbols and the plot,
recorded by Moses, prophets, kings, and priests.
The men listened intently to all he taught,
silently soaking in the biblical feast.

Approaching the village, he spoke of Micah
and Zechariah, of colts and the King,
of a suffering servant and humility.
"Stay with us, speak more to us, don't go away."

Invited in to break bread and drink wine,
Jesus tore the loaf and filled cups to the brim,
"This is my body broken for you"—eyes opened!
They came to believe and know it was him.

Then suddenly he left them, Jesus their Lord.
"He's risen indeed, such plain truth we ignored!
What glorious words, even now my heart burns!
He's alive, he's our God of undiminished returns!"

Divine Paradox
After Philippians 2:6–11

Jesus was born, but he always was, is,
and forever exactly God, Trinity,
the unseeable seen, yet did not exploit his
equality but gave up his kingly
power and privilege to be a servant
to servants, to be humble for the proud,
to die for the dead, to embrace the cross.
The Master obeyed, the king kneeled, the victor
humiliated—but God lifts him up,
way up, above every name so that all
will kneel, all will know, all will see, all will say,
that he is the One who won, our All in All!
Every knee will bow, every tongue confess
Christ is Lord! He is God and nothing less!

Part 4:
Spring Awakening

"My life is like a frozen thing,
   No bud nor greenness can I see;
Yet rise it shall—the sap of Spring;
   O Jesus, rise in me"
                    —*from* "A Better Resurrection" *by Christina Rossetti*

"Grief melts away
 Like snow in May,
 As if there were no such cold thing."
                    —*from* "The Flower" *by George Herbert*

To me: Discontinuity

Come to Jesus—I've heard it before, but now
I hear, "Come *to me*, you who are hungry,
thirsty, needy; come, eat, drink, be filled, bow
the knee, be truly free." He said this *to me*.
I knew there's a God, but not one who bothers
to notice small things, small beings, small me.
I drew close, I drew in, I looked up: He's
infinite, all-powerful, and mighty.
Amazed by God: "Holy, Holy, Holy"
Ashamed by me: "Wicked, Wayward, Wretched"
Crushing, blinding, burning, gasping... Save me!

But then...

Gentle, warm, wounded hands touched me, lifted
me up, washed my dirty feet, gave me wine,
fed me bread. Then he said, "Come, you are mine."

I was lost, blind, but now I'm found, now I see.
"I came to you," he said. "Now come to me."

Augmenting Reality I:
UnPlugged

Among digital crowds, yet quite alone.
I still need daylight though a light can flick on.
Deaf to singing sound without an earphone
Remote control but my control is gone.

I feast on augmented reality,
each course, sans real, still seems to satisfy.
Dainties on demand, devouring 3D.
Tricked by surround-sound, duped by my own eye.

Who can unmute my mouth, cause me to speak?
Who can unplug me, make lips talk, legs walk?
Who's there to really "friend," "follow," "like," "tweet"?
Who can write real words on real rock?

Turn my channel so I broadcast good news?
A thousand channels yet me he did choose.

Augmenting Reality II:
Electric-flame, Hallowed Fire

My life is low res. Space invader, pix-

elated. But not really euphoric.
Minecraft blocks, no-limit lives, a Phoenix
from "ashes to ashes," a poor Yorick.
Breathing but no breath. Bleeding but no blood.
Slumped shoulders, glassy eyes, click a new game.
Fingers on the controls, digital mud,
bitmap sky. My world is a screen, my name
a pseudonym.
          Until... I felt the flame,
the real heat, the felt burn that I can't pause,
can't reset. Fire, impossible to tame...
From before to evermore, from my "was" —
though really "wasn't" —to I Am, who is
the refiner's fire. Ablaze, I am his.

Me, before

In the void of space and time, before space
and time, before breath, blood, sinew and cell,
before me, before it, before a trace
of quarks, atoms, planets, heaven or hell...
Even before foundations founded for
the foundations of the foundations of
the foundations of finite evermore.
A Word was heard, a Thought thought, Three in Love
Although there was no thing, there is someOne.
Three in One—the one and only—Father,
Holy; the Spirit, life-breather; and Son,
Redeemer, Husband, Friend, Hero, Brother
Saviour, Lord, Prophet, Priest, King—yes, of me
he thought, he made, he called. And set me free.

Unbelievable belief given to me

Is it I who believe or is it him
who stirred in me? An alarm cannot wake
the dead. Incessant, honking, buzz can't make
a corpse dance, even with a raucous rhythm.
When blind-healed I saw, when beyond the brim
I drank of him, I know I did not take
the cup; the draught I drank did soothe my ache,
this healing elixir was a gift from him.
I saw no light until I saw him—Yes!
Until he thundered and flashed and called to me:
"Lazarus, Come Forth!"—"Blind man, Look and See!"
Awakened soul, dancing to righteousness,
reborn, renewed, remade, yet fully me.
Incredible creed, believing I see.

Real Ideal

Distant, cold, empty thought—a god of my
idolatry. Silent. Unrequited
love. Idols can't speak, can't hear, unsighted.
Made up word—words. The "Thou," a wistful sigh,
An idea-idol carved from the sky,
moulded with mist, god, an uninvited
guess. The desperate hope. Some words recited
to the corner of the room—and yet I
heard—holy yet here—"Comfort, comfort my
people," says my God. My guilt is taken
away. Eyes, behold your King of beauty!
Ears, be opened, hear how tenderly my
Redeemer—risen, real—says "Forsaken
no more," for my God is reality.

You called

Like Andrew, who left fish and net behind,
hearing my name, so I came. You called me,
invited, harkened, so gracious and kind.
Like Nathanael, you saw under a tree,
so you saw me. Like Matthew, James, and John,
each you made, each you chose: "Come, follow me."
You open ears, open eyes, you beckon
to me, from where you found me: "Hear and see!"
Now that I see the real you, hear your voice,
I proclaim with my mouth, my heart, my mind
Jesus is Lord, the best and only choice.
My words, my walk, my will are realigned,
turning from wrong, on my knees I confess,
given a new life that you richly bless.

Immerse, emerge

My feet step down, deep into the water.
Then my legs, stomach, chest. It's not enough
to baptize part of me. I'm no bather
seeking to wash away mere dirt and stain.
You, Lord, mean to drown me—inner, outer me.
I declare to all, what this means, what you
mean to me, what you are making me to be.
Laid down like a corpse to a grave, out of view.
My watery tomb becomes a new womb,
as though knit anew, remade, raised upward—
reborn, resurrected, ready to bloom.
Rejoice with me, all who see and hear my words.
Those gathered here to witness this display,
now testify that I am what I say.

Part 5:
Summer Light

"Teach me, my God and King,
In all things thee to see
And what I do in any thing,
To do it as for thee.."
—*from* "The Elixir" *by George Herbert*

Beautiful

Beautiful are the feet of those who bring
good news—Lord, make my feet beautiful too.
I heard, now I speak, a new song I sing!
I'm loved, now I love; I saw, now I do.
Though I may be shamed, I won't be ashamed.
I knowingly trade short term grief for long
term gain. Though cast down, my spirit's enflamed,
though silenced and accused, I remain calm.
Wonderful and beautiful are the feet
and lips and lives that bring and sing good news.
The story of one who embraced defeat,
yet it was not the end; he did not lose.
Scarred but beautiful are his feet and hands.
As we tell this truth, his kingdom expands.

from feast to forever feast

Gather around the table, come sombrely.
Lamb's blood, a blood banner, covers the door.
Enter in, come freely, eat peacefully.
Firstborn slain, none need be slain anymore.
Come feast at the table, eat of the Bread,
harvested from heaven, baked in a womb.
The Loaf broken, many pieces are spread...
Life-bread is offered from the empty tomb.
Come and drink the fine wine, poured from one cup:
Blood of grapes, royal and red, crushed and spilled,
deliberately shed. Be nourished, drink up,
this wine quenches our thirst. We are fulfilled.
So, eat, drink, remember, and be merry!
The wedding feast awaits in eternity.

Blood

Life-giving blood from the giver of life,
Lamb's blood protects, watches over our sons.
Sprinkled blood, offered up, a sacrifice,
covering over sins for all seasons.
Blood mixed with myrrh, anointing the High Priest.
Blood mixed with frankincense, so sweet a scent,
beckons and draws us to your holy feast.
Blood mixed with water, a cleansing descent,
baptized, reborn, risen up, and refreshed.
Blood mixed with wine, crushed from the grape, making
hearts merry and fortifying our flesh.
Blood mixed with sweat, with tears, your heart breaking.
And your blood mixed with mine, flowing as one,
making me your brother, co-heir, and son.

Alive here and now

The incarnation declares that matter
matters to God. Jesus did not condemn
living in the world. He came to shatter
boundaries, reorder and upend them.
From this world, Jesus never retreated.
He understood life in "flesh and blood" terms.
He fed the hungry, healed the sick, feasted
with friends; he wore a crown made of harsh thorns,
and he suffered on a real, rough-hewn cross.
Son of Man, fully God and fully man.
His skin, muscles, bones still bear the emboss
of whips, nails, and spear. His nail-hole hands can
be seen, touched and held. New life is given,
abundant life, for here, now, and without end.

Austerity is not a name for God

Austerity is not a name for God.
The monks missed the mark—our God is lavish.
He's prodigal, he's extravagant:

A sunset is just a keyhole glimpse of his luminous loveliness.
A six-volume saga is barely a phoneme in his grand story.
An eight-course spread is hardly a crumb from his banquet table.
The total sum of Bach's musical corpus
        is but a jot and tittle in his marvellous melody

(This is why Jack—ever the grammarian—changes the confes-
sional "and"
to "by")... Our chief end is
        to glorify God
        by
        enjoying him forever.

Boundless
limitless
satisfying.
His joy, our joy;
        his glory, our glory.

He is able to do far more abundantly than all that we ask or think

Beyond imagination.

what you were made for,
what you were born to do—
is to make God's greatness, holiness, loveliness known
          and
to enjoy our great God
          Forever   and   ever.
We need forever because he is infinitely
          en

               joy

                    able.
He is the forever-
                    more. More lovely. So much more.

Change me from Water to Wine

When I look at this glass of red wine
I'm reminded that you turned water into wine.
I'm reminded that you give your blood as wine.
Wine for tasting (that the Lord is good)
and wine for drinking in remembrance of you.
I'm reminded that you make me into wine—
You've turned me from nothing into something.
Like grapes in the press, you crushed me under the weight of your
Holiness—
making me one with each other, one with Jesus.
You drained me, strained me, by the grace of your love,
aged me in your perfect timing.
Made me into fine wine, the best for last.
Make me wine for the world
so that I glorify the Winemaker.
Cause my words and deeds to make merry the hearts around me

I caress this glass of wine, nestled upon my palm.
I swirl the cup,
I breathe in the bouquet—fragrance of fruit,
herbs, flowers, earth, heaven...
The aroma of Christ,
the scent of holiness and beauty and life
and power to transform

May I be intoxicated with you
filled with your Spirit
May I not be ashamed
Take my life, drink me in,
pour me out.

Saturate me with Jesus' blood-wine
deep into my centre
and spread
throughout my body—head, heart, hands,
feet, ears, eyes, lips, and tongue.

I hold up this glass of wine.

I can't see through the dark, purple-red,
a bottomless red sea in a crystal goblet
      but still
      a glimmer of light
      peers through
      like candles illuminating rosy stained glass—
      gentle, constant light—if I could hear light—like a low,
steady hum—
this darkly glowing ruby cup.

There is such mystery in wine, as there is mystery in me.

The miracle of transformation
      from impotent
      to potent,
from water to wine.

Friendship

We've gathered early, as the morning
light peers through the winter woods. A yellow
glow from the nestled cabin adorning
the pond's shore welcomes and invites fellow-
ship and friendship. The crack of splitting wood
echoes across the water, fuel for fire,
warmth for words, spoken in love (for our good)—
and in jest—for our delight! We acquire
wisdom this way, speaking words and the Word
into each other, food for life and soul.
Pipe and tea nearby, voices heard, spirits stirred,
and Prior sings. We drink deep, we depart full.
As iron sharpens iron, so also friends
sharpen friends—such a precious gift our God sends!

Part 6:
Autumn Grace

"Myself, arch-traitor to myself;
    My hollowest friend, my deadliest foe,
    My clog whatever road I go.
Yet One there is can curb myself,
    Can roll the strangling load from me,
    Break off the yoke and set me free."
        —*from* "Who Shall Deliver Me?" *by Christina Rossetti*

I am, so I do

Too often I mutter words to the air.
Sometimes I'm sincere, confessing failing
in despair: "Help me stop!" is my prayer—
But I sin on. "Evil is assailing
me!" I cry. But he says, "Why is the door
left open, friend? I gave you self-control,
the Spirit-fruit. As you are, do. Abhor
what is evil. Flee, resist, be careful
to be what you are. Put off but put on.
Pray for humility, but be humble.
Outwardly do what is inwardly done."
Still, I fear to walk. What if I stumble?
"But passive wishing is still misstepping—
Keep in step with my Spirit by stepping."

Some truth

The Accuser points—"There you go again."
He reminds, "Don't forget what you've done."
It's not a lie, no deception here. None.
Wretched I was, still am, causing much pain.
I thought he deceives, feigning a false stain...
but he's right about me: "A lousy son,
proud husband, selfish man..." he's just begun.
He's a *roaring* lion with fiery mane,
fierce teeth, appetite ready to *devour*
not bite, *ruin* not wrong, *destroy* not harm.
"Be afraid. There's no hope. You don't belong.
Abandon Christ. You've fallen from favour."
But I'll submit to God, trust His Strong Arm:
He is firm and faithful, my hope, my song.

Holy Wind

I

Sometimes I pop my collar to the wind,
tucking my chin to my chest.
Yet cold, wet air still rushes through my sieve-like
coat, sweater, skin, muscle—
My bones shiver.

I tremble because I know the Spirit is here
when the wind blows like that.
Hovering over the water of my unformed
soul, deformed by my downward gaze,
enamoured with earth and
my delusional self-deification
        —sounds silly, but that is what it is.

The Holy Wind will blow. Sometimes he is a gentle
breeze. So very gentle.
Like the soft sound of displaced air
of a mourning dove's fluttering
wings
bringing peace
and joy
when I take notice.

Sometimes he is still.
So I am still.

When first he came he was the Chinook
            —warm, dry wind rolling down from the mountains so sud-
denly—
wicking away tears, sopping up the dampness of my soul,
melting down my ice rock resistance,
eating up snow that once swallowed me—
snow-eater. That's what some call you.

Come warm wind.
Animate my thoughts, my limbs, my life
            re-create me
            renew the ground I walk on, level the earth beneath me
pour Love into my hollow chest
fill me

II

I pray

Rushing wind, blow into me
blow open my eyes—bring me the message from the mountain top
Fill my lungs, aerate my blood and bones
Flood through my larynx
Shake sounds from me
Vibrate my voice to say and sing—
push past my lips, teach me to testify,
cause my mouth to make much of you.

Righting prayer's ship

My words drift toward bare palms. My back bent,
knees against the bench, body bowed, head hung.
Does He hear me, am I really present?
Mind adrift, world too near, a siren song
seeping in, sounding me—I veer off course.
Slumping, slipping, sinking into silence,
a sea of silence. Gone is my remorse
for sins said, sins done, a prayer's pretense.
But then my Lord speaks, at the helm to steer,
Holy book, with charting words, guide my lips.
Written compass, searching truth, purpose clear:
Adore, confess, give thanks, ask… God equips
men to pray, righting our ships with His will
to say, Son to model, Spirit to fill.

Though I forsake

"My God, my God, why have you forsaken
me?"—words spoken by Christ, nailed to a tree,
said by him so they need not be spoken
by me. You are not far; you hear my plea.
My God, my God, why have you rescued me?
I'm prone to wander; I want to look back.
Now with hand on the plough, don't let me be
like Lot's wife, while she fled, yearned to backtrack.
At times I hunger for Egyptian bread,
melons, leeks: food for slaves, though slave no more.
Prevent me from returning to Herod,
for I've seen the True King, followed the Star.
When in your presence I arrive at last
I will know it was you who held me fast.

porneia astrape

I have made a covenant with my eyes:
I will not gaze upon a woman who's not
my wife. I must be a man who relies
on your Spirit in me, on truth taught
that I'm blood-bought. I must do more than flee,
not just run away, but run to you, Lord.
Delighting in you grants me victory,
Yet there are times I'm careless, bitter, bored,
soul feels dry, heart cold. So I click, gawk, gaze.
I seek pleasure in the quickly fading,
fizzling, fake pics, degrading the gifts you made—
sex and love and beauty; I'm left hating
what is right by lusting for what is wrecked.
O Lord, heal, forgive, restore, redirect.

Taking Holy Gore for Granted

There's something gruesome about sacrifice.
Levitical victims, corpses of beasts,
slaughtered, ripped, torn, and bled: a gory price
for wrongs we did; guts sorted by the Priests—
Meat, fat, sinew and skin; bones, brains, and blood.
Lambs, birds, bulls, wailing and wishing to live:
Bleating, flailing, cutting—a crimson flood
pouring out, burning up, no more to give.

We forget the grisly cost paid for life.

Ground beef in grocery stores, shrink-wrapped, white
styrofoam. No sordid sorting, no knife
dripping with guilt. We, too, forget the sight
of blood-encrusted, rusted spikes, so rife
with sin. We nailed them in, into real hands,
this ghastly due that holiness demands.

Sin, Sorrow, Salvation

I.

The preacher said:
> There are two kinds of sorrow that sin brings in this life:

Both are real.
Both come from loss.

> Point one.
> The first sort of sin-sown sorrow (the one that leads to
death)
> is sorrow over loss.
> > loss of reputation

loss of pleasure
loss of liberty
loss of stuff
loss of what we really worship:
the creature not Creator.

> Point two
> Saintly sorrow, godly grief, sadness over sin, comes from
loss too.

The preacher said and I heard the Spirit speak:
> saintly sorrow comes from loss.

I understood. *My* loss of You.

I lost you like losing daylight, like drawing the curtains,
blotting out the Sun,
and hiding hoarded sin in a dark corner of my heart.

But now I grieve as I wallow in the gloom of separation.

My heart breaks over our broken
fellowship, friendship, worship, wonder.
Against You, and You only, have I sinned.

Restore me.
Keep me from sinning ever again. Intervene. Always show me the
way out
from under.
Shine on me again.
Take me in again. Lift me up, again.
I'll pluck eyes, sever feet, sever hands, whatever it takes.
You mean more to me.
Not to earn You but to stop me from losing You again.

II.

You offer fresh fruit, hanging from the tree; but I reached down
I stole the soiled, overripe, fermenting fruit that litters the earth.
I took more than I could eat—sickeningly sweet
bruised, browning...

So I am banished from the garden
but I lost more than the garden. Infinitely more.

I lost You.

Godly sorrow leads to repentance.

I come again to You, Jesus: with You, in You.

I find no good gifts from anyone, nor in anything.
The wrong I do offers only a gift-wrapped grave,
it doesn't deliver; it only delivers me
to loss.

Loss of You.

Against You, and You only, have I sinned.

So this is why I grieve.
I will turn away from offending misdeeds
I will return to You.
And You, You did not take away your Spirit from me.
You come, You give.

Now
        no more sadness,
        no more sorrow.

No regrets, not anymore.

I'd like to say…

I'd like to say I've been pulled down, pulled in
by wicked and wrong-doers around me.
I'd like to think I was coerced to sin,
dragged kicking, screaming, that I tried to flee…
I'd like to blame enemies who conspired
against me, confounded my good intentions.
I'd like to point out the devil desired,
decreed, directed me with deceptions…
I'd even like to accuse you, O God.
But you are not my source of sin: I am.
I willingly oppose you. I'm the fraud.
I've gone astray, like another Adam.
Rescue me from me, defeat my mirror
enemy—restore me, my redeemer.

Violent Winds

I see such violence, not only war,
but violence against all that you made.
Plastic seas, poisoned earth, and trees no more.
Concrete litter makes beauty and hope fade.
I see so much violence against us,
not just killing us—though that happens too—
babes; the old; the dying—even *one* is too much...
It's the death of persons, handmade by you.
We've murdered gender, family, marriage, love.
We've executed Imago Dei.
Suicidal peace, slaughtered joy, grieving dove.
We're free not to be; free not to be free.
Yet I will trust in you: redeem this world.
Please don't delay; we're becoming unfurled.

All this the world well knows
After Sonnet 129

Desire is nursed, a thought becomes hunger,
hunger becomes intent, "want" becomes "act."
Taken pleasure is pleasing no longer—
dust on the tongue, hate-filled heart, guilt-wracked
soul. Like swallowing fish bait with open
eyes, a knowing glance at hook-pierced morsels—
Seeing the glinting barb ready to rope in
and gouge gaping mouths; there are no reversals,
no pulling back once pulled in. Bait and hook
wedged in the throat, a memory of taste,
unswallowed bliss stuck on a devil's crook.
Choice is gone. Alluring thrills now laid waste.
  All this the world well knows, yet none knows well
  To shun the false heavens that lead to hell.

Helpmate

You are a voice, an ear, a soft caress.
My total delight: head, heart, soul, and flesh—
All my earth-bound life, a fountain to bless
needs nothing more, wants nothing less.
You are my wind, sail, and keel, my lighthouse,
my shore, my hearth; you're the storm and gentle
waves. My companion, my friend, and my spouse—
Forgiving always yet in season judgemental,
the heat and the hammer, the coals and ice,
my witness, defender, judge, and juror,
my taker and giver of sacrifice,
my shield-bearer, my admirer, my true mirror.
While I have breath and blood as I walk this sod,
you show me how every good gift comes from God.

A Parent's Prayer

As you have done for Solomon, making
silver as common as stone, so you've done
for us—so rich we're guilty of taking
for granted the gift of daughters and sons.
This quiver full of arrows is given
for such a time, so show us how we ought
to steward these arrows; give us a vision
of Christ and his gospel—one that's lived, taught, caught.
May our God be their God; may your hope be
our surety, strength, and guide. May fears dissolve
(whatever may come) as you cause us to see
your loving embrace, and may we resolve
to hold tight your shield and lift high your sword,
so that all in this house will serve you, our Lord.

Evensong at St. Paul's

I.

In a city of beautiful buildings, here is another,
yet unlike any other: St. Paul's.
We walk, we gaze, we wonder
      is there time?—
The evening is here. Day is closing for the day.

But then a sign

calls us—a literal sign—
invites us to Evensong.

We climb up stone steps, enter in.
Even the small doors seem massive doors,
weighty tomes hanging on brass hinges
that shut out distractions, shut in the distracted.
The walking and talking and busyness and bustle all
become strangely dim. Silence becomes our song.
We are submerged into the stunning stillness.
So much larger on the inside.

Look up, can't help but look up—
a twilight, sky-like ceiling and world-like walls,

so vast yet still too
small.
Even here is too finite for the
infinite
       to dwell.
This man-made place for the maker of man:
the best we can do—this! is barely a droplet of dew.

Outside, we're wanderers in this city, tourists in town, set apart.
We're aliens in—but not of—this urban place.

But in here, inside,
We're now in and a part of this sacred space.

II.

The ancientness. The art. The Faith. I belong here.
Still I feel painfully exposed and alone.

It's humbling to be so small for this brief hour.
God seems so distant here because he is echoed everywhere.
Indeed, we are separated by an infinite divide

but we begin to chant, and recite, and sing, and hear of the One
who fills the boundless chasm, who spans the ever-expanding

space.

Holy words for Holy God; carefully prepared words,
some ancient, some old, some uttered soft, some spoken bold.
Haunting voices rising up to darkness and mystery—

my ears, my neck, my mind, my skin—I feel the sound of truth surrounding
immersing me,
gently washing over me like
the very breath of God.
Words so right and real; this place, so here and now.

God's beauty is seen, the goodness of the Good News is heard—
every note, every utterance, every square inch alludes
to his wonder, his transcendence, his descent, his ascent, his

> nearness,
> his farness.

This is Evensong. This evening service of prayers, Psalms, and singing

> a symbol of unity, harmony
> a paradox of the near farness of God.

III.

Liturgy, ritual, words recited, words sung—

We're reminded that this is a religion as well as a relationship.
    He is Creator, we are created.
    We are together, we are alone.
This is not yet heaven, though it is heaven that this hour harkens us to see.

So, despite the wonder, so much to look at, too much to take in,

I still find myself on this earth. My feet still feel the floor.
My body is still a body, pulled down by gravity of the world
and worldliness.
So the tide begins to rise, the tide of blood, muscle, and bone rises
over my mind, my soul.
My weary traveller's bones — the night of flying, the day of walking,
the hunger for seeing, the desire for doing, and the peace
of this place —
overtake me.

My lids slip down beneath the surface,

    over my eyes,

        like the not-so-watchful three
        in the Garden of Gethsemane.

This edifice, this service, my effort to worship
One who exceeds imagination.

We're always reaching up,

but you, O God,
    must always lift us up.

And you do.

Ecclesia Reformanda

The second law of thermodynamics states

> that everything is breaking down
> moving from order to disorder,
> out of order, from together to
> alienated. Cut off.
> Things fall apart.

Like a new car, fresh off the lot,
already worth
        less: rusting, decaying, depreciating—
The inevitable
        en

                    tro

                            py.
But chaos seems so
dramatic
when describing aging, aching bodies,
or old batteries bleeding energy,
or stars burning out,
or even the church growing cold.
Losing her fire, losing her first love.

Ecclesia semper reformanda

The church is always reforming,
The church must always be reformed.
Not reinvented, not reimagined—
but re-formed:
put back together.

Always re-tuning, always returning
to Christ

    His Word
    His gospel
    His Truth
    Him.

                          When walking the wrong path

            the fastest way forward

      is to turn

back.

Ecclesia reformanda.

The Reading Pilgrim

Bunyan wrote a story about a man
Graceless (such was my name too). He portrays
an ordinary life, an everyman.
Called to walk the Christian path, yet he strays,
wandering wayward, yet also finding
the Way—narrow but clear—and the Gate,
saving him from fiery darts, blinding
darkness, hopeless hope, and the devil's hate.

As I read, Help's hand lifts me from the mud.
As pages turn, so does my turning heart.
I, too, flee the Fair with its wallowing in blood.
My burdens are shed; I'm given a new start.
So as Pilgrim crosses that final river,
I, too, yearn to see the only Life-Giver.

Do you love me?

Jacob said to put away foreign gods.
Moses said, so many times, don't forget
the Lord your God who brought you out of Egypt.
Gideon tore down the Asherah rods.
Jehu struck down the false prophets of Baal
Josiah wept over the overlooked
scrolls rediscovered; he obeyed the book,
repaired the Temple, fixed every detail.
Hezekiah, Ezra, Nehemiah,
Amend your ways, it has been said again
and again. And again. Revelation
calls us back to our first love, the Messiah.
So you ask us repeatedly, "Do you love me?"
yet forgive us (again) for acting faithlessly.

In old age

Colour fades from my hair, my skin, my eyes
like an overcast day in late winter—
a silvery shale bridge between horizon and heaven.

Yet still my head bears a crown

      a crown

like the fiery blaze of orange,
      red, yellow of autumn woods
      before recusing itself for winter's bleak proceedings

like the wide-eyed, mouth gaping
      sight of the setting sun—
      as golden light brushes and beams in the grey-white clouds
      So much beauty
      floods the horizon for one last fleeting moment
      before the shade of night.

What I now know is how little I know, and even less I knew.
What I now feel is that there was more good I could have done
      more words I could have said
      more I should have left undone
      more I should have left

unsaid.

I also know—know!—how God blesses
		beyond imagination
		how he is faithful—rock faithful, ash and grey rock—
		beyond granite and solid-earth faithful,
		beyond belief, beyond certainty.

So, I will
		go gentle into that good night.

Yes, I will
		wade the river

Because of him
I will hear
		well done

Because of him
I will hold
		finally hold my saviour
who has always—always!

held me.

Part 7:
World Without End

"O Lord, make me know my end
and what is the measure of my days;
let me know how fleeting I am!"
—Psalm 39:4

"He will wipe away every tear from their eyes, and death shall be
no more, neither shall there be mourning, nor crying, nor pain any-
more, for the former things have passed away."
—Revelation 21:4

"Death, be not proud"
—*from* "Holy Sonnet 10" *by John Donne*

not normal, not natural

We weren't made for death; it was a path we
chose. Death wasn't made for us—we made it.
Common to us all yet we always flee
this closing of day, this becoming unknit.
When Lazarus died, even Jesus wept.
The "I Am" who spoke of resurrecting—
he knew what he would do for this death-kept
stone-cold corpse (petrified, putrefying).
He also knew this isn't what he made,
not for us—rotting, reeking, body betrayed.
He wept and raged against the abnormal grave.
He said, "Take away that stone!" Though decayed,
he told Lazarus to leave death's borough.
The dead man walked out. "Unbind him, let him go."

A Word to Death

"Death, be not proud," Donne told you. You've been tamed.
Your pride in blood-soaked wood, seeming defeat
of the One you fear most—Yes, what a treat
to take hold of that holy corpse that made
Life and love and light. A tombstone blockade
to our Hope, hope doused in myrrh, no aid
to come, your job was done. But he greeted
you with "It is finished!" —*not* "I am defeated."

Death, be not proud—there is no accolade

Not for you. You are dead because he lives!
An empty tomb, a folded shroud, a scent
of incense, and there, a thorn crown thrown down.
Now he's seated, gold crowned, freeing captives
once rightly yours. O, Death—your ravishment
is complete—He's lifted up and you're torn down.

New Bells

The bells no longer toll for me. Now shout
out, "I heard the bells on Easter morn!" Bells—
sound swells, truth tells—ringing out, singing out,
bringing out—we're released from prison cells!
The lame, the deaf, the blind—now walk, hear, see!
And can it be that I should gain? His pain,
My gain? Book and bell tell of cradle, tree,
empty tomb, sinners free, a new refrain

we now sing, bells now ring, a great Wedding!
To our Bridegroom King we can cling! An endless feast,
the Banquet table, set with wine. We bring
only songs, voices of praise! From the least
to great—we all are princes, royalty:
Robed in his righteousness, eternally.

Sources for Epigraphs

Donne, John. *Devotions Upon Emergent Occasions.* Ann Arbor: University of Michigan Press, 1986.

———. *John Donne: The Complete English Poems.* Edited by C.A. Patrides. New York: Alfred A. Knopf, 1991.

Guite, Malcolm. *Parable and Paradox.* London: Canterbury Press, 2016.

Herbert, George. *The Temple.* UK: Penguin Classics, 2017.

Lewis, C.S. *Mere Christianity.* New York: Touchstone, 1996.

Milton, John. *Paradise Lost.* Edited by William Kerrigan, John Rumrich, and Stephen M. Fallon. New York: Random House, 2007.

Rossetti, Christina. *Christina Rossetti: Selected Poems.* London: Orion Publishing, 2003.

Shakespeare, William. *The Tragedy of Hamlet.* Toronto: International Thomson Publishing, 1997.

Terpstra, John. *In the Company of All: Prayers from Sunday mornings at St. Cuthbert's.* Toronto: The St. Thomas Poetry Series, 2016.

Appendices

Appendix A
How to read a sonnet

"A Sonnet is a moment's monument
    Memorial from the Soul's eternity
    To one dead deathless hour..."
    —*from* "Its Functions" *by Dante Gabriel Rossetti*

I have written mostly sonnets in this collection. The sonnet is a centuries-old form of poetry that emerged during the Renaissance. Like 14th-century architecture, art, and sculptures, the sonnet captures an essential artistic ideal of the Renaissance: creativity abounds within the tight limitations of technical beauty. The sonnet is fourteen lines long, with ten syllables per line and it has a fixed rhyme scheme. The restriction on syllables and lines causes the shape of the sonnet to appear on the page like the ideal shape of a golden rectangle.[12] This ideal shape conveys not only beauty but perfect proportion.[13]

---

[12] The golden rectangle draws its dimensions from the golden ratio (*Phi* ratio: "a+b" is to "a" as "a" is to "b"); this ratio frequently appears in nature (e.g., a fern coil, sea conch, or pine cone, the pattern of hurricanes, even the milky way). The golden rectangle was an intentional feature in much of the artwork and architecture created during the Renaissance. The ratio, sometimes referred to as the Divine Proportion, dictated the arrangement and proportion of statues, rooms, and painted scenes. A single sonnet with its fourteen lines and ten syllables per line can appear on a page like a rectangle made with the golden ratio.

[13] This insight came to me while reading Malcolm Guite's "Introduction" to *Sounding the Seasons* (Norwich: Canterbury Press, 2012), ix–xvi, as well as John Hollander's "Foreword" to *Sonnets* (New York: Everyman, 2001), 17–19.

The most famous Italian sonnet writer is a man named Petrarch. We often refer to the Italian sonnet as the Petrarchan sonnet after him. This form of poetry follows a fixed rhyme scheme and basic structure as follows:

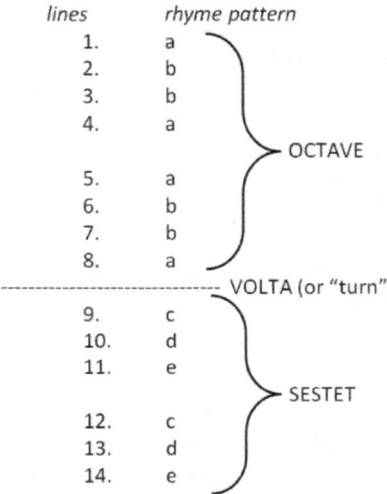

lines	rhyme pattern	
1.	a	
2.	b	
3.	b	
4.	a	OCTAVE
5.	a	
6.	b	
7.	b	
8.	a	
		VOLTA (or "turn")
9.	c	
10.	d	
11.	e	SESTET
12.	c	
13.	d	
14.	e	

The first eight lines—the octave—usually introduce a problem; this problem is a disconcerting conundrum that the poet or speaker is experiencing. After the octave, the poem *shifts* by taking a "turn" or a "volta." This volta may consist of a change in tone, perspective, attitude, or the poem may be progressing toward a resolution. The remaining six lines—the sestet—is intended to convey this shift to the reader. Many Petrarchan sonnets address the speaker's desperation while in the throes of unrequited love, as he adores and admires a silent woman on a pedestal. I have used this model for a number of the "pre-conversion" poems because I felt it captured the sense of isolation we feel when we refuse to acknowledge our Creator. We wish that there is a God, and we are angry because we think he isn't there. The irony is, of course, that the seemingly silent God on a pedestal is the one whose love is unrequited by us; God is really there, and he is not silent.

The second form of the sonnet was invented by the Earl of Surrey, who brought the sonnet into its current English form during the

English Renaissance. The English sonnet was then made famous by the great playwright William Shakespeare, who wrote dozens of astonishingly brilliant sonnets. The English sonnet (often called the Shakespearean sonnet) consists of the following pattern of three quatrains and a concluding couplet:

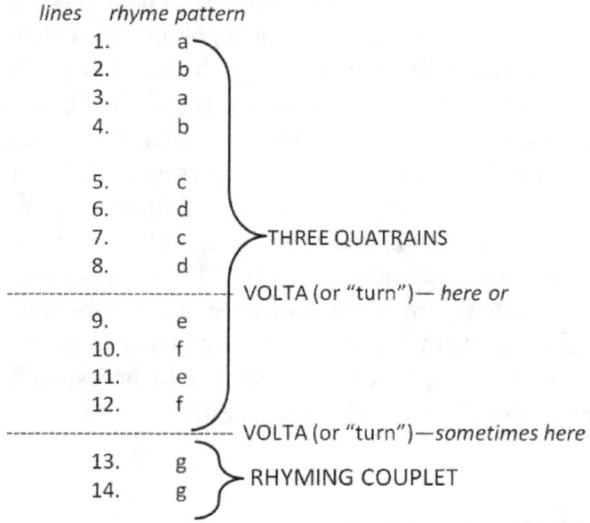

Similar to the Italian sonnet, the English sonnet follows a pattern of introducing a problem and then shifting into resolution; after the first ten lines (or sometimes eight lines), there is a shift in tone, perspective, or attitude that leads toward a resolution.

The sonnet is a marvellous form of poetry because it is short enough to be readable, especially in this present-day context of sound-bites and 140-character tweets. The sonnet is also marvellous because the structure itself captures the nuanced tensions that exist in Christian theology and life. Our God is the God of great shifts and unexpected paradoxes. For example, we are both body and soul... we are saved by grace, yet faith without works is dead... we are chosen by God, yet we also choose him... God is sovereign, yet he is not the maker of evil... God is just, yet he redeems unjust people... and so on. These turns and tensions are well conveyed within the sonnet structure.

Although the sonnet is an older form of poetry, I have attempted to avoid archaic vocabulary and unnatural rhythm and rhymes. For the most part, I have stuck to the limit of ten syllables per line, although I have not forced my verse to adhere strictly to the rhythmic pattern of iambic pentameter found in Shakespearean sonnets.[14] This collection of poems is not intended to be a series of pastiche poems for memorializing poetry from a golden age. I want these poems to be read and understood by people here and now. Occasionally I veer into other forms of poetry, such as the villanelle, the elegy, and concrete poetry.[15] I also employ the free verse form because it conveys the unravelling that can occur in a person's life. Rosaria Butterfield once described her conversion to Christianity as a "trainwreck."[16] Her conversion dramatically upended her life, career, and relationships. The metaphor is apt—Christ breaks into your life when you become born again. Conversion is a dramatic upheaval, just like physical birth. So at times, I also tried to capture this upheaval not only through free verse but also by occasionally breaking the patterns established by the sonnet form.

---

[14] "Iambic pentameter"—an iamb (pronounced /ˈɪˌam(b)/ with a silent "b") is a combination of two syllables, with one unstressed syllable followed by a stressed syllable. Here is an example of an eight syllable iambic line, with capital letters representing the stressed (emphasized) syllables: "if ALL the WORLD were AP-ple PIE." Pentameter simply means there are five iambs per line. Here is the first line of Shakespeare's famous Sonnet 18; notice it contains ten syllables and five iambs: "Shall I | com-PARE | thee TO | a SUM |-mer's DAY?"

[15] A villanelle is a complex 19-line poem involving two repeated lines and only two rhyme sounds. A masterful English villanelle is Dylan Thomas' "Do not go gentle into that good night." An elegy is a lament for the dead, often honouring their achievements and mourning their loss. The classical elegy uses elegiac couplets, but many elegies may have varying forms. A concrete poem uses the arrangement of the words on the page to help convey meaning visually. One of the best concrete poems is George Herbert's "Easter Wings."

[16] Rosaria Butterfield, *The Secret Thoughts of an Unlikely Convert* (Pittsburgh: Crown & Covenant, 2012), 25.

Appendix B
Making sense amidst the chaos

Creation itself begins as words. In Genesis, God speaks the universe into being (or sings, as C.S. Lewis might have imagined it[17]). With his words, God brings *form, function*, and *meaning* into creation. Out of the empty void came all things as God imagined it. The universe, we are told, is "without form and void and darkness was over the face of the deep" (Genesis 1:2). Then God speaks: "'Let there be light,' and there was light. And God saw that the light was good. And God separated the light from the darkness" (Genesis 1:3–4). God's creativity involved sorting and differentiating one thing from the other. When God created Heaven and Earth, he created order out of chaos.

We are now commissioned to continue the creative process, cultivating the world and making new beauty (Genesis 1:26–28). Since we are made in the image of God, we also have a desire to create in the way God himself creates; this does not mean we can create *ex nihilo*—out of nothing—but it does mean we have been made with the desire to move our surroundings from chaos to order. For example, God's commission to Adam to name all of the creatures God made is humanity's first way of ordering the environment and sorting out what is what. It is also humanity's first creative act (Genesis 2:19). Adam invents the names himself.

Since the beginning, understanding our world through words has been central to our creative and cultural mandate as humans made in the image of God. It should be no surprise, then, to see that poetry

---

[17] C.S. Lewis describes the creation of Narnia in *The Magician's Nephew*. In the chapters called "The Fight at the Lamp-post" and "The Founding of Narnia," Aslan is heard and seen singing the world beyond the wardrobe into existence. I wouldn't be surprised if God's voice sounded like "the most beautiful," "harmonious" and "triumphant" music ever heard when he spoke the universe into being.

has always been a process of creating order out of chaos. Making sense in a seemingly senseless world has a long history in the annals of literature. From Homer's *The Iliad*, written as Ancient Greece exited its own dark age, to Virgil's *The Aeneid*, which helped usher in "Pax Romana," to Milton's great English epic poem *Paradise Lost* born out of the crucible of the English Civil war. During WWI amid the frenzied and unstable conditions of trench warfare, poets like Siegfried Sassoon, Wilfred Owen, and Robert Graves, sought to make sense of the horrors of war and convey these experiences poetically to the English-speaking world. Although WWI was not the "war to end all wars" as was hoped for, it is John McCrae's Great War poem, "In Flanders Fields," that still resonates with us as we attempt to come to terms with modern military conflicts that still plague nations around the world. Rich poetry also emerged during the unrest of the American Civil Rights movement. In times of turmoil, poetry is often an essential tool for navigating the chaos of life on earth.

A biblical example of a poet seeking to make sense of his world amid chaos is young David while on the run from King Saul. Fleeing for his life and trying to survive in the unforgiving wilderness as an outcast and outlaw, David hid in the Cave of Adullam, and he wrote poems. Many of the poems David wrote while in exile appear in the Book of Psalms.[18] Although the Holy Spirit uniquely inspired these psalms, David's skill of writing poetry was a talent that he likely honed while passing the time as an isolated shepherd boy tending his father's sheep. Like playing the harp, poetic prayer was one of the ways David used his gifts to manage the challenges of his life. We still turn to the psalms in our present times of challenges and difficulty, to read them, meditate on them, and pray those words back to God.

Poetry is born out of chaos, and it brings us comfort when we are surrounded by the chaos of life. This is why poetry is the oldest form of human writing and has dominated the literary world for millennia, with works like *The Epic of Gilgamesh*, *Beowulf*, Dante's *Divine Comedy*, Spencer's *Fairie Queen*, Milton's *Paradise Lost*—just to name a

---

[18] See, for example, Psalm 13; 35; 52; 54; 57; 59; 63; 64; 108; 142.

few. This is also why poetic hymns have meant so much to the church, especially in times of persecution, and why the poetry of Negro spirituals grew out of the trauma of race-based slavery in the United States.

We live in chaotic and unsettled times again. Such times require poets and hymn writers to help us see God's plan and purpose written into the fabric of our current age. Poetry reminds us there is still beauty in times of disorder. Poetry also reminds us of the power of words, especially those of prayer and God's word. We need to continue the creation mandate to cultivate order and beauty amid the chaos and ugliness of our surroundings. Like David and so many others in times of uncertainty, we need poets to hunker down and write words of comfort. We need poets to once again point us to the Great Poet himself, the "God of all comfort" (2 Corinthians 1:3).

Appendix C
Poetry, microwaves & Big Macs

"I hate poetry!" English teachers hear this phrase every time they mention the "p" word. Poetry has become synonymous with words like "confusing" and "pointless," or phrases like "out-of-date" and "hard-to-understand." If this rings true with you, then let me change the subject for a minute...to twenty-first century Western culture.

We like our communication fast—texts; we like our food fast—McDonald's; we like our cooking fast—microwaves. Our culture is filled with services and devices that provide ease and speedy convenience. As a result, we have come to expect everything to be fast, easy, and just-a-click away. Our collective cultural "attention span" is becoming shorter by the second: when surfing the internet, for example, the average viewer will spend fewer than 5 seconds on a webpage before clicking away. The problem with "fast, easy, and convenient" is the accompanying lack of depth, vitality, and longevity. Few of us cherish emails the way we might cherish a handwritten note or letter; few of us remember the last fast-food meal or celebrate the microwave meatloaf the way we remember and celebrate Grandma's turkey dinner or homemade pie.

So what do emails, Big Macs and microwaves have to do with poetry? These icons of cultural convenience have very little to do with poetry, other than to serve as a stark contrast: poetry is anything but fast, easy, or convenient. So why should Christians bother investing time and energy into understanding poetry? Because poetry helps us to slow down, ponder, and understand the deep and profound realities of God's universe. While our culture is chock-full of vapid, ephemeral experiences, God's creation is full of inspiring, rich and eternal experiences. "Be still," the psalmist writes, "and know that I am God" (Psalm 46:10). In our fast-paced, non-stop, 24/7 culture, reading poetry teaches us to slow down and "be still." Poetry instills in us the habit of remembering and reflecting on who we are, who God is, and what life is all about.

Poetry is also a powerful way to express the wonder, depth, and beauty of God's world and to capture the essence of our human experience. Nowhere is this more evident than in the poetry of the Bible. The great poems of the Psalms have been the mainstay of many Christians through times of trial and joy; the depth and profundity of the Psalms are in part due to the medium of poetry. This is true with hymns as well; Christians cherish the poetry of hymns sung weekly during church meetings. But our enjoyment of poetry should not be limited to psalms or to hymns. All great poets are great observers; they hold up a mirror to ourselves and to society, so they have much to teach us about life on earth. In a powerful way, they urge us to stop and reflect on our human experience, God's universe, and his goodness to us in a world mired in sin.

As we read a broad range of poetry, both secular and sacred, we will be challenged to look at ourselves and God's world with fresh perspectives. Our ability to appreciate the Psalms and hymnody will also be enhanced by concerted attention to all kinds of poems. Most importantly, perhaps, we will learn to pause in our hectic lives in order to take in the beauty and wonder of God's creation.[19]

---

[19] This essay is reprinted from Jeremy W. Johnston, *All Things New: Essays on Christianity, culture & the arts* (Kitchener: Joshua Press, 2018), 59–61.

Scripture Index

130

131

132

133

134

136

Acknowledgements

Although writing is a solitary business, a book like this does not appear on its own. Paul tells the Corinthian church, "For the body does not consist of one member but of many." Indeed, many friends and supporters stood behind this project. I would like to acknowledge and thank a few of the key players who helped this collection of words and scribblings transform into this volume of poems you now hold. I first must thank Chance Faulkner and Corey M.K. Hughes, my publishers at H&E, for their willingness to print a book of my poems. Poetry books are rarely best-sellers, so I'm very thankful for their support. I especially want to thank Chance for embracing this project early on. His frequent check-ins and words of encouragement, and his timely and sage advice were an invaluable catalyst to bringing this book into being. I thank God for his love for Christ, for his friendship, and for his firm conviction that these poems will be useful for edifying the church and furthering the kingdom of Christ. I also want to acknowledge Melissa Poremba, who is not only a highly valued colleague and copyeditor, but also a cherished friend. I'm thankful for her willingness to engage in the (near impossible) task of copyediting a book of poems. I greatly value her meticulous attention to detail and her excellent suggestions for improvement. I have endeavoured to amend all the errors, incongruities, and weaknesses she diligently uncovered; if mistakes still remain, then the fault is entirely my own.

I would like to thank Doug Sikkema, Benjamin Inglis, Karen Swallow Prior, Andrew Roycroft, Leland Ryken, and Malcolm Guite for taking precious time to read my book and write such generous and kind endorsements. I am in your debt.

Thanks to Paul McCallum, a poet in his own right, for enriching my heart, soul, and mind on countless occasions. In his company—in the backwoods cabin while enjoying the plentiful gifts of God—much of my thinking on matters of life, faith, and the arts took form and provided the foundation for the poetry now collected here in this volume. Thanks, also, to my friend and mentor, Peter Pikkert, for his welcome advice, gracious prayers, and unending support of this project. Peter is a kindred soul who regularly reminds me to be the man that God has made me to be, and to see my writing as an important ministry to the glorious church of Jesus Christ. I would also like to express gratitude to my pastor, Hagop Tchobanian, for his Christ-centred preaching and his faithful ministry at my home church, Pilgrim Baptist Fellowship. The Lord has used Hagop's preaching to transform my heart and life in countless ways, and many of those sermons have inspired poems in this volume. Thanks also to my friends and fellow authors, Ruth Tchobanian and Benno Kurvits, who provided helpful advice on the cover design for this book.

To my fellow wordsmiths and brothers-in-ink—the Blind Bards Literary Society—I offer my gratitude for listening to some early versions of these poems and providing valuable feedback and encouragement. Long live the potato!

A big thanks to my loving and supportive family, who have been such a blessing to me in so many areas of my life. I thank God for my parents Glen and Wil, parents-in-law Lorne and Carolyn, my sister Melissa and her husband Derek, my brother Jeff and his wife Laura, as well as my nieces and nephews. Their reactions to my writing have always been positive and cheerful, especially when I foist poems upon them. I also thank God for my children. Joseph, my eldest, is my in-house English scholar who provides academic street-cred for my poetry. I'm so thankful for his literary mind and his enthusiastic support of this project. My second son, Nate, was the first person to hear about my foray into the world of poetry. His heartening reception enabled me to persevere in this endeavour. I am also thankful for his incredible artistic talent in providing me with an outstanding author portrait for this book. My two daughters, Katie and Abby, are my muse and my constant delight; in particular, Katie's boundless creativity and Abby's insatiable curiosity have inspired me to write so many of these poems. I thank God for the blessing my children are to me and for their love and admiration. I have dedicated this book to them in hopes that they will gain a richer and deeper knowledge of Christ and his gospel.

My wife Laurie remains my most stalwart and longsuffering supporter. She is my earthly compass and inspiration for all that I do, and the poem "Helpmate" is written as a testimony of all that she means to me. She is a gift from God, "more precious than jewels" and "most beautiful among women" (Proverbs 31:10; Song of Solomon 1:8). To my beloved I say, *is ceol mo chroí thú*, Irish for "you are the music of my heart."

Lastly, to Christ, in whom I live and breathe and have my being... My finite gratitude cannot do justice to him who is the fount of all that is good and lovely. To him be glory, forever and ever! Amen!

About the Author

JEREMY W. JOHNSTON is the author of *All Things New: Essays on Christianity, culture, & the arts* (Joshua Press, 2018) and he is the arts columnist for *Barnabas* magazine (SGF Canada). When he isn't writing poems, blogs, or columns, Jeremy teaches literature and history at Hillfield Strathallan College and Mohawk College. He and his wife, Laurie, have four children and they live in Hamilton, Ontario, Canada. For more information, please visit **www.jeremywjohnston.com**.

Author portrait by Nate Johnston

"So teach us to number our days
that we may get a heart of wisdom."

—Psalm 90:12

ALL
THINGS
NEW

Essays on Christianity, culture & the arts

Jeremy W. Johnston

Date Completed	Name

H&E *Publishing*

WWW.HESEDANDEMET.COM

CPSIA information can be obtained
at www.ICGtesting.com
Printed in the USA
BVHW071411080321
601998BV00002B/238

9 781989 174616